I0392667

LEADERSHIP

TIPS FROM 10 SUCCESSFUL AND WEALTHY PEOPLE ABOUT LEADERSHIP AND MANAGEMENT SKILLS

By

Mark Grant

Copyright © 2016 by Mark Grant. All rights reserved.

No part of this publication may be reproduced, distributed, or transmitted in any form or by any means, including photocopying, recording, or other electronic or mechanical methods, or by any information storage and retrieval system without the prior written permission of the publisher, except in the case of very brief quotations embodied in critical reviews and certain other noncommercial uses permitted by copyright law.

TABLE OF CONTENTS

INTRODUCTION

If you observe carefully, you will notice that the most successful entrepreneurs in the world possess a common set of virtues, which can help them to remain on top of their game. Most of these virtues pertain to managerial and leadership skills, and understanding them can give you a head start.

These virtues can be developed and will help you improve your leadership skills, which in turn will help your business flourish and get the right dues.

This book contains comprehensive leadership tips and tricks that will usher you into the right direction. You will get the best advice out there from the best in the business and avail handy advice from 10 of the most successful people in the world.

So without much ado, let's begin!

TIME MANAGEMENT - TONY ROBBINS

Life coach, Tony Robbins, believes that it is important for people to dedicate enough time to feed their minds with information that will help enhance their time management and leadership skills. However, most people end up denying themselves such vital information by being too busy.

People often waste their time while performing mundane activities such as commuting, running errands, cooking, etc. Although, these are inevitable parts of life, it is important to manage time in the best possible manner. He stresses on the fact that time management is vital when it comes to increasing productivity. If you while away your time and expect to remain on top, then it will not work out. You have to make the conscious effort of utilizing time to your advantage.

He believes in the concept of 'N.E.T Time' of No Extra Time Time. This refers to utilizing the time when you are physically busy but not mentally. Suppose you are cooking and have an easy dish to prepare - instead of fully focusing on the dish, you can instead think of inspiring and informative things to make the most of your time.

Even if you spend just 30 minutes per day, gathering useful information, then you can vastly improve your knowledge. But remember, it is just as important to implement the gathered information, as the mere acquisition is useless. You should know to practically apply all the information that you gather.

Find Yourself - Mark Cuban

It's no secret that Dallas Mavericks owner, Mark Cuban, is an efficient leader. Here are some useful tips that Cuban provides about time management and leadership:

• SET YOUR OWN PATH

If you wish to be a leader, then you have to set your own path and not follow the pack. Mark says, "Leaders don't conform to the consensus. They create a consensus to their vision and goals". A true leader will carve out his own path no matter how difficult it gets. Many obstacles will come in the way, but you must patiently make your way through them to reach your goal.

• STAY FIRM

Regardless of how tough the going gets, a good leader is one who does not move away from his stance. Mark says, "Leaders don't change their positions mid-debate. They welcome scorn from the masses because it creates the opportunity for dialogue". Even if there are a hundred people questioning your decision, as a leader, you have to stick with it till the very end.

• FORGE AHEAD

A good leader will not delve into the past, but will only look forward. It is important for you to forget about the past and focus on the future. Mark says, "Leaders don't look backward to condemn what has already been done, they look forward to creating a better future". Even if you have made blunders in the past, you have to forget about them and look forward to not repeating the same mistakes again.

• *WALK THE TALK*

It is important for you to put your principles into practice and not simply talk the talk. Mark says, "Leaders are not dogmatic. They are principled and know that change is never easy, but when it's necessary, they must lead".

INVEST IN YOUR PEOPLE - WARREN BUFFETT

Billionaire businessman and entrepreneur, Warren Buffet, has extensively written about what drives him and his business. Here are some tips on management and leadership from the mogul himself:

• *GOOD COMMUNICATION IS KEY*

Buffet says that good communication is one of the key elements of being a good leader. It is not enough to just have a plethora of great ideas; it is paramount that these ideas are shared with the right people. Those that communicate well enough manage to become better leaders.

• *CHOOSE WISELY*

A good leader will choose a good set of people to work with. It is important to identify each employee's caliber and pick the ones that will work best with you. Once you choose the right candidates, you have to manage them efficiently in order to attain the best results.

• *FUTURE PLANS*

Buffet says that it is important to pick the next generation of leaders and train them to become like you. He says, "The primary job of a board of directors is to see that the right people are running the business and to be sure that the next generation of leaders is identified and ready to take over tomorrow."

Technological Innovation - Steve Jobs

One of the greatest entrepreneurs of the 21st century, Steve Jobs, managed to teach the world a thing or two about great management and leadership skills. Here are some of his noteworthy tips:

• SIMPLIFICATION

A good leader will simplify things in order to make it easier for others. For example, Jobs extensively worked on the iPod to do away with the on/off button as it simplified the usage of the device. He didn't care that he had to put in extra hours of work, as long as it contributed towards enhancing the device's simplicity.

• CONFIDENCE

It is important for any leader to be as confident as possible. Confidence was the driving force behind's Steve Jobs' achievements and what every leader must try to emulate in order to attain the best in their life.

• SURPRISE

A true leader springs up surprises from time to time. Be it the addition of a new feature to an iPod or the classic, "one more thing" gimmick that Jobs used during his presentations - people would always remain at the edge of their seats in anticipation of the revelation. This proves that it is important for a leader to keep the audience guessing before surprising them – the guess factor creates that anticipation.

PEOPLE FIRST - RICHARD BRANSON

Virgin mogul, Richard Branson, has an easy approach to leadership and management. He believes that it is important for people to understand and make use of the three "L's" of leadership that are as follows:

• LISTENING

Branson says that listening is the most important trait to possess and believes that his company has succeeded because of this very virtue. It doesn't matter who is speaking, as long as you are attentive, you will have the chance to pick up on important information that will help you at some point in time.

• LEARNING

The second virtue is to learn. A leader must never stop the process of learning and acquire as much knowledge as possible. It doesn't matter where the learning is coming from as long as it adds value to the leader's skills. It is important to turn to inspiring people to learn some new and inspiring ways.

• LAUGHTER

Branson believes that it is vital for a person to enjoy whatever he or she is doing in life. A good leader will take up any challenge without a frown and laugh his way to success.

LEARN FROM YOUR PAST - OPRAH WINFREY

Oprah Winfrey, one of the most successful entrepreneurs in the world, and also the only woman on this list, has inspired several generations of people.

Here are some leadership advice from Oprah herself:

• *A LEADER NEVER FAILS*

Oprah believes that failure makes a leader stronger and in fact, no bad experience should be considered as a failure. A leader will always look back at his experiences and learn something from it. If you enjoyed the process, then, regardless of the outcome, it is well worth the effort.

• *VISUALIZE*

It is important for a leader to envision his success. You must look at your future self and envision having attained success. That is a sure shot way of reaching your goal. Write down your goals and individually visualize having attained them; this will make the journey smoother.

• *HUMBLE*

It is extremely important for a leader to be as humble as possible. Even if you have attained a lot of success, it is important for you to remain as humble as possible. Oprah had the most watched daytime television show for more than a decade and yet she never stopped being humble. She always had her feet on the ground, which helped her achieve immense success.

THINK OUT OF THE BOX - JEFF BEZOS

Amazon.com founder and CEO, Jeff Bezos, is an extremely skilled leader. Here is some managerial advice from Bezos to ponder over:

• UNCONVENTIONAL THINKING

Jeff Bezos' unconventional leadership style is what has made him a popular figure. He challenged the existing norms and introduced unique ideologies. Bezos started amazon.com to sell books, which was not the standard practice at the time. His future thinking made him and amazon the world leaders in their particular field.

• PLAN FIRST, ACT NEXT

There was a time in the 90's when the leaders would plan 30% of the time and try to sell their strategies 70% of the time. But this strategy must be reversed in order to attain the best results. The leader must plan extensively and then go about implementing the plan.

• WORK BACKWARD

A good leader will first analyze the ending and then work his way backward. This is important, as it will be easier to come up with feasible solutions to problems. It is vital to keep the end goal in sight and then pursue it backward.

Evolve Constantly - Arnold Schwarzenegger

The Former California governor, Arnold Schwarzenegger, has had a diverse career. Right from being a bodybuilder to a movie star, he has smoothly transitioned from one career to another.

Here are some leadership skills that he possesses:

• *DIVERSITY*

Diversity is an important skill for a leader to develop. A leader should be able to do many things and move from one activity to another without having to put in too much effort. However, don't do too many things at one time, as it can cause you to make mistakes. Arnold knew that he cannot be a body builder all his life, and so decided to become an actor and then studied to be able to become a governor. A leader has to put in efforts to set himself up for a future achievement.

• *AIM FOR THE HIGHEST*

A leader must aim at the highest possible goals. Nobody thought that Arnold would ever become a politician. But he always aimed higher and went after everything he desired. Similarly, you too must aim at higher goals and pursue them individually.

• *EDUCATE*

A good leader will take it upon himself to educate others. If someone isn't aware of something or needs help in understanding a topic, then the leader must step up to the plate and provide the necessary education and advice for that person.

BELIEVE IN YOURSELF - ELON MUSK

Elon Musk is one of the brightest young leaders in the world. Having set up multi-billion dollar businesses, he has carved a name for himself in the world of business.

Here are some managerial skills that Elon swears by:

• *PERSUASIVE*

Elon believes that it is important for a leader to be as persuasive as possible. He should be able to get others to listen to him and follow in on his commands. Many Tesla employees have called Elon a strict authoritarian who is extremely persuasive in his approach. It is part of what makes Tesla a great company to work with, and also one of the most successful automobile companies in the world.

• *OPINIONATED*

Elon says that it is good for a leader to be opinionated. The leader should not hold back from speaking out his heart. If you have an opinion about something that is happening within the company then you must voice it without thinking of the consequences. It will only lead to appreciation.

• *CHANGE YOUR MIND*

Don't be afraid to change your mind at the last minute. If you think your decision will work well for you and the company then you must go ahead with it. It is said that Musk often changes his mind on projects and it turns out great in the end.

Even if he has made people work on something for a year; he will change his mind about it at the very last minute.

LEAD FROM THE FRONT - MARK ZUCKERBERG

Facebook founder, Mark Zuckerberg, is a popular youth leader. Many potential entrepreneurs who wish to follow his footsteps look up to him.

Here are some leadership tips from Mark:

• *PASSION*

A good manager or leader should be passionate about his work. Even if you have the most boring job in the world you have to find a way to enjoy it. You should fuel passion into every single aspect of the business in order to attain success. According to Zuckerberg, "Find that thing you are super passionate about. A lot of the founding principles of Facebook are that if people have access to more information and are more connected, it will make the world better; people will have more understanding and more empathy. That's the guiding principle for me. On hard days, I really just step back, and that's the thing that keeps me going."

• *ARGUMENT*

A good leader will always be up for an argument, and not adversely react to his decision being questioned. Those bosses that refrain from understanding another person's opinion, end up losing out on the chance of improving themselves and availing useful solutions to existing problems. A good leader owns up – whether the situation is good or bad.

CONCLUSION

I thank you once again for choosing this book and hope you had a good time reading it.

As you can see from the personalities covered, management and leadership go hand in hand, and a good manager will always be a good leader and vice versa.

If you apply the tips shared by these successful personalities in your life, you will be able to become a better leader and manager. I hope you find the success you seek by using this advice and better your managerial and leadership skills on a personal and professional front.

ALL THE BEST!

NAVY SEALS
Self-Discipline

**TRAINING AND SELF-DISCIPLINE TO BECOME TOUGH
LIKE A NAVY SEAL**

INTRODUCTION

You might have heard about Navy SEALs, but do you know everything about what they do? A quick background will help you get a better understanding.

Navy SEALS are one of the most elite group of fighters in the world, but there is so much more to being a SEAL than fighting. They do operate in a world that's far different from our own, but their training can prove to be a useful weapon in your arsenal for achieving success.

QUICK BACKGROUND

In the year 1962, under the orders of President Kennedy, the United States Navy had established a special sea, air, and land team known as Navy SEALS. The Navy SEALS are considered to be an elite group of specialists who are trained to engage in unconventional combat. High-impact missions that require stealth—which cannot be carried out by large forces like tanks and submarines—are carried out by the SEALs. For all the operations that either start or end in water bodies like swamps, oceans, coastlines, and so on, the go-to team of specialists for Navy, Air Force, and even Army Special Forces would be the SEALs. Though the Navy SEALs belong to the naval unit of United States, they are trained to engage in missions on all types of terrains and extreme climatic conditions as well.

This book contains proven steps and strategies on how to train yourself mentally, physically, and emotionally like a Navy SEAL to achieve your goals. Well, it is likely that you won't be on par with the well-trained SEALs but you can definitely make use of their principles in your day-to-day life.

CHAPTER ONE: TRAINING REGIMEN OF NAVY SEALS

MIND OVER MATTER

The human body is made up of many different organs, but the brain is considered to be the most powerful of all. You wouldn't be able to perform even the simplest of functions—like moving your muscles—if your brain wasn't functioning. You might have heard stories of heroism performed by men on battlefields that saved not just their lives but also of those around them. They wouldn't have been able to do so if they weren't mentally strong. Navy SEALs are trained in such a manner that their brain can override their physical pain and push them to function in a manner that would usually seem impossible. Mental preparation is the key to unlocking your true potential.

The brain is a muscle, and you will be able to train it by engaging in some mental exercises. You can do these mental exercises any time and place. You can exercise your mind to unlock your potential by engaging your mind in the following exercises.

Battle-proofing will help you to condition your mind to react in hostile situations and emergencies, by developing mental strength for managing a crisis. This can be done by visualizing intense fights. When you start battle-proofing your brain, it will start believing that you have experienced all that you have imagined. Whenever a similar situation comes up, you will be able to take quick action.

You will need to create your own "triggers." A trigger is something that can help you ignite the qualities that are necessary for not just your survival but for your personal growth as well. Your trigger could be a memory, a phrase, or an experience that can move your mind and soul towards achieving your goals.

You should train your mind to get out of situations that would stress you out unnecessarily and this will help you to gain control over a situation.

Navy SEALs are trained not to act on the first impulse that pops into their mind, but to consider all the possible ways of acting in a critical situation. You will be able to do this only when you can reign in your thoughts and control your mind.

When you are truly aware of your insecurities and true motivations, you will be able to avoid making the same mistakes again and can move forward. Understanding the purpose behind your job, whether you are a Navy SEAL or not, will help you excel. Learn to make yourself as happy as you can be in any given situation and don't do anything halfheartedly.

Have faith in yourself, surround yourself with positive company, always focus on the present, and don't live in your past or future. Lastly, learn to control your breathing. Navy SEALs are tough men, not just because of their bodies but because of their minds as well.

VARIOUS STAGES OF TRAINING

Warfare preparatory school

The training curriculum for becoming a Navy SEAL starts at the Naval Special Warfare Preparatory School referred to as NSW Prep, in Great Lakes, Illinois, and lasts for 8 weeks. The aim of NSW Prep is to prepare the SEAL candidates to endure the grueling physical trials of BUD/S. NSW Prep ends with a PST that you must pass if you want to become a SEAL. It begins with a Physical Screening Test and ends with a grueling PST that includes a 1,000 yard swim to be completed in or under 20 minutes, 60 curl-ups in 2 minutes, 70 push-ups in 2 minutes, 10 pull-ups in 2 minutes, and a four mile run with shoes and pants that needs to be completed within 31 minutes.

BUD/S Training – 3 phases

BUD/S stands for Basic Underwater Demolition/SEAL Training, and this helps to develop the physical and mental strength of the candidates who want to become Navy SEALs. BUD/S lasts for 7 months and has different phases that test the physical, emotional, mental strength, and also leadership skills of the candidates. BUD/S has a three-week orientation, followed by the three phases mentioned below.

Indoctrination:

This lasts for three weeks, and introduces the candidates to the BUD/S lifestyle at Coronado: the Naval Special Warfare Center. The INDOC is designed to help prepare the candidates for the training they have to undergo in the three phases.

Phase 1: The first phase lasts for seven weeks and it assesses the SEAL candidates in different areas of physical conditioning: proficiency in water, teamwork skills, and mental strength. Physical conditioning includes swimming, running, and calisthenics, and the course grows harder every week. The first two weeks of this training prepares them for the third week, also referred to as "hell week". The candidate has to take part in five and a half days of strenuous training with maybe 4 hours of sleep for the entire week, and the training can exceed 20 hours a day. After the "hell week," the remaining 4 weeks are spent learning different methods of creating hydrographic charts and conducting various hydrographic surveys.

Phase 2: This lasts for 7 weeks and is the diving phase, aimed at training and developing the SEAL candidates' skills as combat swimmers. The physical training becomes more intensive and focuses on combat scuba. It focuses on open as well as closed circuit scuba. Basic medical training and dive medicine skills training is given. This phase helps make sure that the applicants are capable of making use of swimming and diving techniques as transportation from their basic launch points. If a candidate wants to complete the second phase, they would have to showcase an extreme level of comfort and ability to perform in stressful and tough circumstances.

Phase 3: This lasts for 7 weeks and trains the candidates in land warfare like the usage of basic weapons, land navigation, demolitions, patrolling, rappelling, and small unit tactics. There is a lot of classroom work that teaches them to read maps, use compass, and to collect and process information for completing their mission. These skills allow the candidates to become more comfortable while out in the field.

For the last three and a half weeks of the training, the class is taken offshore to San Clemente Island. Here they get to practice all the skills that they have acquired in the third phase. The training and work becomes more intensive in order to mirror the work they get in field. This is the most intensive part of training, because the training goes on for all seven days of the week with minimal sleep, while handling dangerous explosives and ammunition. Also, the punishments for mistakes at this stage of training are extremely harsh.

Parachute Jump School:

After the completion of BUD/S the SEAL candidates proceed to San Diego, California to learn static and free fall training at Tactical Air Operations. This is a 3-week program that is conducted by highly trained and qualified instructors and it is designed to help transform the SEAL candidates into competent free fall jumpers within a short duration of time. At the end of the training they should be able to complete night descents in all their combat equipment from an altitude of at least 9500 feet.

Graduation

The SEALs training concludes with the BUD/S class graduation, where the candidates who managed to survive the grueling training stand proud in their Navy uniform and receive the pins with the Trident insignia, the symbol of becoming an official Navy SEAL. The achievements of the new SEAL recruits are recognized in the presence of various senior SEAL leaders, Senior advisors of Naval Special Warfare groups, Naval Commanding Officers, other SEAL teams, and family members.

Post-graduation training

The SEAL training doesn't end with becoming a part of the SEALs. Even after graduation, they continue to be put through extensive training before they are sent out into the field on missions. The BUD/S was just a qualifying training program and it is only after continuous training will they be qualified as SEALs officially. Once the recruits have been assigned to a particular SEAL Team, then their troop training begins. This is pre-deployment training, it can last from 12-18 months, and is divided into three phases that include: individuality specialty training, unit level training, and task group level training.

The training that they go through is extremely tough and testing on the body, mind, and spirit. Going through it might not be possible for all of us, but we can definitely implement a few of their practices in our daily life for becoming more successful.

WHAT IS NAVY SEAL SELF-DISCIPLINE AND WHY SHOULD YOU LEARN FROM THEM?

The reason for this is simply, training like a Navy SEAL will make you more confident in yourself. When you are mentally, physically, and emotionally strong, you will never feel incapable of achieving something that you want. You needn't be a Navy SEAL in order to win, you just need to adopt a few of their principles.

PHYSICAL FITNESS

Being physically fit and in shape does go a long way when it comes to boosting your self-confidence. This might sound vain, or even superficial, but it's the truth. Training the way that SEALs do will definitely help you achieve great physical strength and fitness.

MENTAL TOUGHNESS

Most of the battles that we face in our life are mental or emotional. The SEALs are considered to be amongst the world's physically superior specimens, but their mental conditioning is just as important as their physical superiority. Most of the time, it's mental trauma that cripples them. Only those who are mentally and emotionally fit can survive being a SEAL. This will also make you a confident person.

SITUATIONAL AWARENESS

Being aware of yourself and the situation you are in can help a great deal when you are on the path towards achieving your goals. You shouldn't have any illusions about who you are and what you are doing. Always be sensitive to your surroundings and this will help you figure out exits and different strategies for getting yourself where you want to be.

QUICK ACTION

Being able to take quick action in a situation of crisis is extremely important for the SEALs. In the situations they usually find themselves in, even a small mistake or delay can prove to be life threatening—not just for themselves, but for those around them as well. You can condition your mind to act in a certain manner in a specific situation and when the time comes, your mind will automatically do what it has been programmed to do instead of wasting precious time figuring out a course of action.

Chapter Two: How To Develop Self Discipline the SEAL Way: Part I

Through Improving Physical Fitness

Due to the extremely demanding situations they have to face, Navy SEALs always have to stay in their finest physical shape if they want to carry out their missions successfully. Navy SEALs need to be in good cardiovascular shape, nimble, strong, and quick. Cardio and calisthenics are the most important aspects of their physical fitness programs.

Cardio

Navy SEALs usually have to disembark really far from shores in order to approach the enemy territory as stealthily as possible. At times they need to swim great distances with their weapons and gear on. Well, if you swim, you might realize that swimming in a pool for 10 laps can drain you completely, but if you have to swim with all the added weight of your weapons, that's really tough. You needn't swim 1 kilometer in the open sea or run 1.5 miles under 11 minutes while wearing your army boots, but doing cardio regularly will help you to stay in great shape. Cardio helps to increase your heart rate and improves the delivery of oxygen to the various muscles in the body to burn out all the fat. The most practical way of doing cardio is running. You just need a pair of good running shoes and you are set. The only limitation that you will have to overcome is your mind. Swimming, cycling, and even jogging are good forms of cardio.

Calisthenics

Bodyweight exercises are an extremely important part of fitness regimes, and calisthenics helps you to stay in shape without building any excess muscle. When it comes to combat, functional strength is the most important factor that you should take into consideration. Lifting strength and functional strength are extremely different. For example, scaling a wall requires functional strength and not lifting strength—a gymnast would be able to scale a wall easily when compared to a bodybuilder who can pull down 400 pounds! Grip push-ups, pull-ups, bodyweight back extensions, squats, lunges, jumping squats, sit-ups, crunches, planks, burpees, trunk twists, and so on are good calisthenics exercises. You can start out by working three times a week and increase it to four to five times a week. Make sure that you are working out all the muscle groups and not overdoing it.

Yoga

Yoga is extremely good for developing mental and physical strength. Your mind will become more alert and you will feel yourself getting stronger spiritually as well. There are different yoga poses that you can do depending upon the part of the body that you want to work on. Breathing exercises will help you to calm your mind, and ensure the optimum supply of oxygen to various parts of your body for their better functioning. Anulom vilom, kapalbhati and Bhrastrika pranayama will help you regulate your breathing. Yoga poses like tree pose, cobra pose, triangle pose, shoulder stand pose, plough pose, bow pose, fish pose, forward bend, downward dog, and child's pose will help in developing core strength.

Running

Running is an important part of Navy SEAL training, and you will need to concentrate on form and effort to improve your running potential. If you want to build your stamina, then long slow distance would be the most ideal style to start with. Agility is extremely important for SEALs because they need to traverse great distances on foot and run around a lot while carrying all their ammunition and gear. Running at a consistent, moderate pace for long distance will improve your stamina greatly. Continuous high intensity running is tough, but it will help you achieve and maintain a great speed for a longer duration of time. You can also adopt high intensity exercises combined with short intervals between them, like cross fit.

THROUGH IMPROVING NUTRITION

Aside from performing all the rigorous activities and exercises that the SEALs have to, they also need to have nutritious food daily. When it comes to physical health as well as fitness, nutrition plays a very important role. You might have seen people who regularly and religiously work out at the gym and still look like the Michelin Man. This is because of their poor diet that's full of sugar and fats.

Diet plan for the whole day

Navy SEALs have a very demanding job and for them, having nutritional meals is very important to keep performing well. Navy SEALs follow NOFFS (Navy Operational Fitness and Fueling Series) for maintaining optimal nutrition. The NOFFS limits the consumption of processed foods and encourages the consumption of whole foods that are good for the body. High carbohydrate and protein consumption along with fiber is extremely important for SEALs, for maintaining their strength and stamina.

For good metabolism, SEALs eat small and frequent meals. They eat about 4 to 6 meals every day with a gap of at least two hours between each meal. This prevents binge eating and helps burn calories as well. This is a good way of eating, not just for the SEALs, but for everyone in general.

Consuming carbohydrates the size of your fist, proteins the size of your palm, dietary fats the size of tip of your thumb would be sufficient for a normal person.

A Navy SEAL would have his first meal before working out at 6:00 a.m., and it would include something that has a little fat content to keep them going, like an omelet made of egg whites and 2 slices of wheat toast. Eat as many grains as possible, but avoid white bread and pasta.

The second meal would be at 9:00 a.m. after working out and consumption of carbs is permitted now. This will help in the transportation of insulin throughout your body after the workout. 2 bananas with a glass of milk with reduced fat content, or oatmeal with raisins and skim milk is a good option as well. You can always add a fruit if you are hungry.

The third meal would be around 12:00 p.m., and this would be your lunch. Avoid oily and fried items as well as the stuff that you find in the vending machines. You can consider having a whole wheat wrap or sandwich with turkey in it and as many vegetables as you like except those that are high in carbs. A few baked potato chips would be good, and broccoli to maintain your fiber intake. Also, you can have a fruit or some yogurt for desert.

At 3:00 p.m. you can have your fourth meal that can consists of a can of tuna or some egg whites on a whole wheat bagel, or a slice of bread. Something light to keep your energy levels up and your hunger in check would be a good idea. Low fat yogurt and vegetables would be good too.

The fifth meal should be consumed around 5:00 p.m. and you can include something really light, because you would consume your dinner in a few hours. Have a small salad or a snack like wheat crackers to nibble on. A glass of fruit juice, protein shake, or even coconut water would make you feel energized. But avoid fat at all cost; you wouldn't want to regain all the fat that you burnt while working out.

The sixth meal for the day is dinner; have it at around 6:30 p.m. Include multigrain pasta or anything else that gives you some carbs and proteins, a little bit of bread, and some protein in the form of chicken or turkey breast, fish, or a really lean stake. Add in as many vegetables as you want and some greens to make a complete and healthy meal. Give yourself at least two to three hours before heading to bed so that your stomach can digest all that you have consumed.

Healthy Eating – Quick Tips

Here are some tips that you can keep in mind if you want to eat healthy every day, just like Navy SEALs:

• You can consume 5 to 6 meals every day that are spaced out with an interval of at least three hours between each meal. Consume small meals and don't binge.

• Don't skip your meals and make sure your diet is rich in protein, some complex carbs, and a little bit of fat as well, but not processed sugar. Eat till you feel full, but don't stuff yourself.

• Remember to exercise every day; don't skip this step. You needn't undergo the rigorous physical regimen followed by SEALs, but do exercise.

• Drink lots of water and keep yourself hydrated throughout the day. Drink some water before every meal and also after every meal. Keep a few healthy snacks on hand whenever hunger and cravings creep in.

• You should always chew your food well and don't swallow it without chewing. Don't starve yourself; eat regularly if you are having small meals.

Chapter Three: How To Develop Self Discipline the SEAL Way – Part II

Through Overcoming Fear

Fear can be crippling. If you overcome your fear you will be able to think clearly and you will be able to tackle the problem at hand in a better manner. But if you let your fear get a hold of you, then the outcome won't be positive. SEALs are trained in such a manner that their brains wouldn't let fear creep in. If you can also train your mind in a similar manner you will be able to discipline yourself and focus on your goals.

Habituation

The reason why SEALs are fearless when compared to other human beings is because of their training, and a psychological technique that is referred to as habituation. This is the process of exposing a person to things or situations that he or she is scared of, repeatedly. Repeated exposure will help the person to overcome their fears, because they start getting used to them and will be immune to it. This is a case of mind over matter. One of the primary weapons of the modern army are the minds of people who comprise it. For becoming a successful Navy SEAL you not only need to be physically fit but also mentally strong.

Setting Goals

Setting short-term and very specific goals will help you perform better. Set small goals that you know you will be able to accomplish with a little extra effort. When you complete or achieve a goal, it will fill you with a sense of accomplishment that will help you in not only performing better, but it will also improve your confidence and boot your morale. According to studies conducted by neuroscientists, the trainees who set short-term goals managed to have a higher rate of success than those who didn't. This technique can be used by anyone, not just the SEALs. Don't bother yourself with what might happen after you have completed the task. Instead, simply focus on the task at hand.

Visualization

This is a technique that is frequently used by sportsmen and even musicians when they want to improve their skills. Whenever they take a break, they visualize themselves as either performing or playing a piece of music perfectly, or swinging their bat really well. Practicing mental visualizations is as important as performing the task itself. During the training sessions, the SEALs have to don their scuba gear and perform emergency drills while underwater. All the while they might keep getting harassed by their instructor who would make the drill tougher by cutting off their oxygen supply or tying up the scuba pipes. In such a situation, they need to keep their calm and practice visualization, because this helps the brain to automatically switch to the mode where it does everything for achieving the goal on hand without much trouble. This is an incredible motivational technique that will definitely help in performing better. Your mind will want to experience the joy it experiences when you visualized the completion of the task, and this will push you to achieve the goal that was set.

Positive Self Talk

Did you know that you talk to yourself at a rate of anywhere between 800 to 1,600 words per minute? That's a lot, isn't it? Imagine if you engage in a negative conversation with yourself for 5 minutes, you will have said around 4,000 negative words to yourself. Well, that doesn't sound fair to you. Navy SEALs are taught simple techniques of self-hypnotism that help them overcome all of the negative thoughts, and instead helps them to focus their energy on positive thoughts and actions. This would act as a motivational factor and help them to move along when the going gets tough.

THROUGH DEVELOPING SITUATIONAL AWARENESS

Situational awareness is of great importance, especially for the Navy SEALs because they are often in such risky situations where one wrong move might prove to be fatal for themselves and all those around them. You can also improve your self-discipline by working on your situational awareness by doing the following.

Arousal Control

Being able to control your state of mind is a very important factor for the Navy SEALs. There are different knee-jerk reactions that are hardwired into our system and fine-tuning them can be quite difficult. For instance, sweaty palms and shaky hands are common symptoms of being scared or nervous. These are natural bodily reactions that are designed for helping you stay out of trouble. This is something that cannot be controlled, and is caused by strong hormones, like adrenaline and cortisol. Controlling the secretion of these hormones is also hard when you are stressed or scared. Navy SEALs are required to perform in extremely demanding circumstances and it is extremely important for them to control these knee-jerk reactions. Practicing deep breathing helps to control your reactions and clear your mind.

Waiting Patiently

Patience might not come easily, but it is a very important trait if you are a SEAL. You will need to be patient and you shouldn't rush anything without thinking things through. Your first thought or impulse might not always be right. There might be alternative ways of doing a single task; go through the possible list very patiently without rushing. This will help you in making the best decision. Impatience will just push you to make rash decisions that could harm you and all those around you. Learn to be patient and you can start to discipline your mind.

Controlling Breathing

Taking deep breaths is also a very effective relaxation technique and it also helps you to think clearly so that you don't make a hurried decision that can be potentially damaging. Whenever you feel that you are panicking, take a few deep breaths and close your eyes. This will help you to calm your mind so that you can think clearly once again without the veil of panic clouding your vision. A Navy SEAL needs to learn to think clearly even in situations of distress, and this skill will definitely come in handy.

Close Observation

Observational skills are very important, and developing them is no easy task. Whether you are a civilian or not, it takes a long time to develop these skills. For SEALs it is extremely important to develop their observational skills because it would help them in their survival! It becomes really difficult to develop this skill when you are a civilian, but it can be done by playing a simple game. The awareness game is something that will help you to develop your observational skills easily. Whenever you are outside, notice little things about those around you and make a mental note of what you observe. When you go home, recollect what you observed and compare the same with what others observed. In a life-threatening situation, like when you are stuck in fire, noticing and remembering a fire exit will definitely come in handy.

Self-discipline is important in every aspect of life, regardless of whether or not you are a Navy SEAL. It helps to control your impulses and to achieve the goals that you have set for yourself by taking the right course of action. When your mind is disciplined, there is nothing you cannot achieve.

CONCLUSION

I hope it was able to help you to understand the qualities that make Navy SEALs tough, and that you can also start training like them: physically, mentally, emotionally, and also nutritionally to become more confident. You might not become as tough as an actual Navy SEAL, but you can definitely achieve your goals by making use of the same principles.

The next step is to apply whatever you have learned in your life, as soon as possible. This will definitely help you change your life positively. Don't rush through these things. Take your time and implement these things slowly.

Thank you and good luck.

ABOUT THE AUTHOR

Hi, I'm Mark and here's a little about me:

I'm an entrepreneur, internet marketer, author, life coach, professional speaker, fitness enthusiast, and world traveler. I feel extremely blessed for the life that I live.

I bring 7 years of niche expertise in self-help and personal development. I'm a business management graduate and I like to study people who appear to be unbeatable against all oddities or challenges of life. I seek answers for failures, lack of growth and thus I want to help people reinvent themselves. I believe: Each and every person is the sole controller of his/her life. If you do not take an utmost care of your life, no one else will.

ONE LAST THING...

If you enjoyed this book or found it useful I'd be very grateful if you'd post a short review on Amazon. Your support really does make a difference and I read all the reviews personally so I can get your feedback and make this book even better.

Thanks again for your support!

www.ingramcontent.com/pod-product-compliance
Lightning Source LLC
Chambersburg PA
CBHW071830200526
45169CB00018B/1305